DOMAIN

DOMAIN

BARBARA NICKEL

POEMS

Published in 2007 by
House of Anansi Press Inc.
110 Spadina Avenue, Suite 801,
Toronto, ON, M5V 2K4
Tel. 416-363-4343
Fax 416-363-I017
www.houseofanansi.com

Permission is gratefully acknowledged to reprint excerpts from the following: (p. vii) Excerpt from Part I of "East Coker" in Four Quartets, copyright © 1940 by T. S. Eliot and renewed 1968 by Esme Valerie Eliot, reprinted by permission of Harcourt, Inc. "Dich wundert nicht .../You are not surprised ...", from *Rilke's Book of Hours: Love Poems to God* by Rainer Maria Rilke, translated by Anita Barrows and Joanna Macy, copyright © 1996 by Anita Barrows and Joanna Macy. Used by permission of Riverhead Books, an imprint of Penguin Group (USA) Inc. (p. 81) "Lily Dale." Copyright © 1996 Christian Burial Music. All rights reserved. Used by Permission. Every reasonable effort has been made to trace ownership of copyrighted materials. The publisher will gladly rectify any inadvertent errors or omissions in credits in future editions.

LIBRARY AND ARCHIVES CANADA CATALOGUING IN PUBLICATION DATA

Nickel, Barbara Kathleen, 1966-
Domain :poems / Barbara Nickel.

ISBN: 978-1-4870-0009-7

I.Title.

PS8577.I3D66 2007 c811'.54 c2007-900428-8

Library of Congress Control Number: 2007921131

Cover design: Bill Douglas at The Bang
Cover photograph: Saskatchewan Archives Board: R-B 5549-IO
Author photograph (p. 94): Paramount Portraits
Text design and layout: Ingrid Paulson

We acknowledgefor theirfinancial support of our publishing program the Canada Council for the Arts, the Ontario Arts Council, and the Government of Canada through the Book Publishing Industry Development Program (BPIDP).

For

T.N.
D.N.
D.N.
C.N.

Houses live and die: there is a time for building
And a time for living and for generation
And a time for the wind to break the loosened pane.

—T. S. ELIOT

Summer was like your house: you knew
where each thing stood.
Now you must go out into your heart
as onto a vast plain. Now
the immense loneliness begins.

—RAINER MARIA RILKE

CONTENTS

MASTER BEDROOM

The mirror's cracking silver would have saved.
It resembled thorns. Beyond that bramble
in the glass, a forest—curtains severe
and green, a deep closet—loomed untouchable.
What happened there the mirror memorized:
Mother smoothing the spread. A sheer fold
of drape swaying, lulled, as she left. A maze
inside those curtains for the girl who holds
escape a possibility, who shatters
bone years later and, strapped and locked, appeals
to a square of sky again. The doors were shut.
A finger on the mirror now, I track a pale
design that keeps me out—a girl obscured.
The only way to touch her is to hurt.

House

Feel the old brick. Chipped. Not really red.
Veranda, vines, the balcony. Gentle
Cyclops with its attic eye that leads
us home from school, watches the antlers
plough the sky each Christmas; our life threaded
through its stare with sparrows, who build lintels
in the vines. Inside, we build our fires,
hundreds, searing our seer, born of fire.

The ruins of its birthplace north of town,
east of that road to the nuisance grounds. Concrete
debris and, in the weeds, brick chunk with THERN
embossed in its hollow. Those sloughs were pits
where men dug, whistled, followed long trains
of thought—the war and wheat and cigarettes—
wiped sweat, shovelled clay into carts hauled
by mule to the yard. Stone wheels, the maulers,

ground clay to bits of memory—a worm
once slurred its heart; a root had kissed. Some vastness
kneaded, dashed into a mould, pressured
to remove air. Heat here, for drying, could cost
a man eleven pounds a day. Formed
brick, flipped and set on edge, erased
the whorls of fingertips from those gloveless
touching it day after day to make a living.

Here stood the kiln. Held up by gravity,
hundreds of brick circles inside circles
mortarless, concentric families
pressing each other into the miraculous
dome. Heat trap. A dozen fires. Degrees
unbearable reached by continuous
stoking. Dark work, shovelling coal and ash,
like fuelling hell. After cooling, they pushed

cartloads of hardened brick outside. Emerge
my home, this pretty edifice. I lie
awake listening to the storm it forged
(thunderbolts hammered for Zeus, the eye
lighting my room at intervals) and furnace
noise of its workshop: creaks and sighs
and blows of operations far below—
trident, helmet, for me, a bow and arrow.

Who Lived There

(Mrs. H.)

My goodness, why on earth? But since you ask
let's see... your old house... clinic... what a task
you've set. Pull up the blind. Is it still there?
I'm almost blind, you know; that orangey blur
is brick I've watched so long it's hard to sort
who lived there when. But yes, an odd neighbour,
before your time, was sickness. Patients climbed
the wobbly stairs looking to cure a limb,
diseases of the heart, various ills.
The way over was fraught with obstacles—
enormous drifts, hazardous icy path,
those stairs (ridiculous!) close to collapse.
Winter, I'd bring a little company
to the receptionist. Poor dear, so many
times I watched her lug the pail of slops,
struggle to the outhouse up the back slope.
Summer, the weeds grew up this thick. Thistle,
was it? Inside grew other fears—a rustling
in the walls (I was told bats), cold forcing
itself through cracks (they rarely lit fires),
all the dark wood. Bare. Behind curtains
shifted the shapes of... well, I wasn't certain
who, they were too far away. That girl
worked by herself a lot; blizzards swirled

around her lonely desk. I've said enough,
I think. Why should *you* care about this stuff?
To tell the truth, I don't remember half.
It was a makeshift place, unkempt, unsafe,
but then—my mind these days—I can't be sure,
just like your house there in the rain seems to totter.

The Doctor and the Doctor's Wife

He touches pain so she can buy the meat
delivered to the house in boxes labelled
Dr. Mrs. before her name. She mixes
hamburgers, her hands sticky with flesh
and fat he barbeques yawning; the phone
woke him at 3 a.m., he dressed in darkness,
drove to treat a cold. He feels a prisoner
in this town sometimes—infections, births,
snowdrifts, complaints, infections backing him
out of winter's garage (the car unplugged
plugged in) into the spring's late muck and back
to this last warmth of fall where lost in thought
he spills some ketchup on his shirt. She's never
ill. She's scrubbing at the stain before
they go to bed. Throws in a load. The machine
(a sturdy chamber) will pump under their sleep,
all day, all over town the houses run
on cycles of wash and rinse and spin. She's never
done. Going upstairs, she notes the awkward
little shelf—(and ornament, an ivory
head)—in the crook of the banister. She'll dust
but until then it's like an itch between
her toes; the house with all its places only
she has felt is a body she's trapped in
although, really, she's in and out a lot;
this afternoon she supervised the Candy
Striper Tea, He mounts the stairs. Today
he touched a bruise, a wart, a man's eyelids
just dead still warm—he reaches for
his wife. In the dark where two can make room
they touch. It hurts. She's crying. I begin.

My brother's wedding ring

clinked on the steering wheel of the old station wagon
as he drove north to our cabin for his honeymoon. He told me
he noticed this because as a kid, sitting in the back seat of the same
car, viewing out the window the same but younger blur
of pine, he'd heard Dad's ring clink like that. I can see
my brother then—

sandwich-making, arm-twists, the eight-track playing
Dr. Seuss and The Beach Boys, howls, giggles, threats
of being made to run behind awhile and that gas-plastic-mustard smell
heating up by late afternoon, I can see him, a pearl diver
under all of this, pulling up from his quiet
realm,

a clink. This came to me the other day
as I was sprinkling dill into the borscht because my brother's ring
had been my grandfather's wedding ring in post-revolutionary
Russia and was most likely steamed by borscht—
the ruble almost worthless, typhus, drought, famine and bandits
looting everything

but a few potatoes for the borscht.
I've read these things in Uncle John's self-published translation
of my great-grandfather's sermons and papers,
thick with historical notes and photos of the murdered
Mennonite families (the rows of well-dressed
bodies in coffins)

which holds a certain cachet, the handwritten
pages smuggled from Russia by my emigrating
family, the book listed in the Acknowledgements
in the hardcover edition of a best-selling, award-winning,
Canadian historical novel. Still, it says
nothing

about Grandpa setting off hungry
for Alexandrovsk that day in June 1921 in search
of rings, his stomach rumbling with the train over the arms
of the Dnieper (viewed on a map, they hold
the Island of Chortitza crookedly, the way he'd bid goodnight
to her) into

the clang and soot of the city where, as the sky was beginning to din
his panic setting in and still no rings, in a glass case,
bed of velvet, the pink gold—pink for the copper that reduced the pri
slid up his finger and would slide up the finger of his wife, board
the *Bruton* (Mennonites filling an ex-military ship)
and cross

the Atlantic to find the surfaces of a new
life: metal, wood, soil, grain. Ties Grandpa spiked
near Wymark, Saskatchewan, no doubt heard
the ring, along with select Low German swearing, never used othe
in the heat (stinking, sweating, unbearable) of 1924. Soil of Great 1
too poor,

too dry, too utterly dusty, crumbled past
the ring, spring after spring. Present on the frosted night
of my father's conception, also at spankings throughout his boyhood,
the ring glints from the pulpit in scripture, in prayer. My father, doctor
at his father's bedside, holds the hand, feels for the pulse, the ring
smearing

the sky with copper. He lets it go. Over the phone just now Dad
informed me (casually but with certainty) that Grandpa,
in contact daily with tractor, threshing machine, seeding
machine, manure, butcher knives, pig insides, cow
insides, chicken wire, horse rope, etc., in fact
never wore

his wedding ring. This was confirmed by Uncle John
who, in spite of having last night fallen asleep
at the wheel causing him to roll his car and fracture
his T8 backbone, was able to vouch, in spite of his aging
memory, with confidence that Grandpa never wore the ring.
Nothing

now but a clink against a steering wheel,
my brother heading north in love with the woman beside him,
the radio on, light rinsing the car so all he can do
is squint at highway line after line pulling him forward
and he can't even see
the rear view.

Former Inhabitants, c. 1917

It seems no one is home, but wait—
one tiny, inner room is lit.
Each night, all lights but one go out
it seems. Is no one home? But wait—
way in the back, she sews, he writes.
Watch, as in the house's heart
each night unfold: her seams, his wait
for the tiny, inner rhyme to light.

GIRLS' ROOM

The *Veiled Virgin*, Giovanni Strazza, c. 1840-56. Marble.

The only way to touch her is to hurt—
to shatter her glass chamber with a fist,
to lift a marble veil falling in perfect
folds down the eyelids, nose, to seek a face
hidden by stone, revealed through stone, apart
from stone, yet stone. Hours pass. Her eyes downcast,
as if to keep from view the child she knew
ecstatic on a mother's lap, that crest
of mountain snow capping laughter. Basins filled
with melt that seeped back into air she breathed,
and didn't fear. What came? The room is still.
Her face, chiselled for years, won't show the heave
down rock of water. It clots her lashes.
We view the pure white falls, not what is crushed.

Salmon Cove Point

Come to the summer house that overlooks
Conception Bay. Upstairs, a cross-stitch sampler
under glass contains a girl's brown lock,

an epitaph. She died at twenty-four.
No one knows how. Come to the window, watch
her fingerprint spiral into a staircase

for her inner curtain's towers, each
designed to be sealed from castle wall in case
of siege, one hundred extra masons required

in the third year to speed progress. Stones hauled,
cartload after cartload from the quarry
of her mind. She didn't sleep. See the holes

in the storm door. The wind kept her up
in battlements, raging through slits narrow
enough to let an arrow fire and still keep

the archer safe. Open the door. Follow
the path she took on fine days to the point.
Horse, sea, meadow red with sorrel,

varieties of moss, lilac and ice plant
escaped from her, as if sensing how sorrow
constructs a dungeon: into the rock a room

was cut, reached only through a trapdoor,
one slit for light. Her culprit would dream
of tunnelling into a wall he'd mortared,

and find his slap of sand and lime impenetrable.
Sit on this rock. Seek the Painted Lady
flitting above the tide pool. In her trouble,

she fixed its wings—colour, design—between lead
cames, changed butterfly to glass
for the apse of her chapel, pulled tapestries

of beach pea from the rock to hang on trusses
in the great hall. To the edge. The sea
here foams like dogs around the moat, her last

defence. Look down. She chose the lichen throne,
the marbled water seething, released
always through holes in stone; began her reign.

Heat

Record highs, the landlord's kids
in the tree house. The deck's our private box;
I'll set the fan closer—a little breeze might
stop your fussing.

They're playing hard; wet hair,
T-shirts drenched in sweat,
and now the girl is screaming
at her brother—I *hate you*—
fair skin purpling; bottleneck rage.
Enter Oma to swat
and yank her offstage...

Still not asleep. Stroller ride?
We'll go around the green
with the church inside. I'll pull
the cover down to keep you
from the sun. Not a person
in sight. So calm and bright,
marigolds in their immaculate
beds. Our village replicates
an Old World model, where even
cows, after pasture, turned
without a struggle
to their master's gate.

Revolution burned that
inside out.

Which is why we're here
in the clean, white heat
going round and round;
Sleep, baby, sleep...

Acrobats at the Circus Fernando

Pierre Auguste Renoir, 1879. Oil on canvas.

Angelina

For our contortions: oranges
I gather as Sister begs more.
Who held these orbs
in his pocket as we torqued
ourselves into hoops? Bored,
I watch the peel decorate
my skin with tiny diamonds. Adore
us, please. We'll take all your
gifts and roaring from this ring.

Francisca

We're dressed alike as oranges.
We do as Papa orders.
Later, in the stale corridor,
he'll make us peel them for
him. I prefer them soaring
like this or juggled with fire
in Grandmama's room, airborne
from her palms, her sideboard
heaped with the fruit she hoards.

First Light Saw Sister

Was there a pig, peeing, strapped belly-up
to the bike's back? A woman balancing
one foot on her bike seat, baskets balanced
fifteen high? Did sand cradle our sleep,

absorb the cold of childhood's deep? How deep
had people tunnelled in the war to make
a home? Did all that we own fit on our bikes?
Did we wear hats like roofs, slanted, to keep

heat running off like rain? What colours rained
as we sped by—snake scribbles, red chilies,
rice spread to dry, white silk moths, peanut hills,
kids' hands waving goodbye? Did people's names

climb like music, were *songs* the long rivers
with water buffalo and mist whispering
our names at 5 a.m.? Did mist in wisps
hold up the mountain we came down, when shivers

danced me ill? How strong were you, to lean
me into bed and make me well? First light
saw sister after sister down the highway; I
was happier than I've ever been.

Road Trip

The vet drives past a bull

up on its hind legs
humping a cow in the early morning,
frost on the newly seeded field.

In the back, her daughters write
a collaborative sonnet.

She thinks how huge and stupid
this bull against
the spring's wheat and silver.

It rhymes, one daughter says.
The other says, it stinks.

Fenceposts

drown in the slough,
red-winged blackbirds
flying off.

A Room

She warns her daughters
to be careful of ticks
as they pick through dry grass.
In the clearing a killdeer
feigns injury, sounds her alarm.

They collect stippled snipe feathers
a coyote left after the feast, touch
cow bones—pelvis, vertebrae tinged
with blood the colour of rose hip...

She remembers the round:
Rose, Rose, Rose, Rose,
Will I ever see thee wed?

Bones in a grove. Maples curved, the backs
of women at work, back of the vet drawing
distressed calves into the air.
Curved to make a room,
its ceiling a swarm of swallowtails.

Valley of Secrets: Museum

Here, long ago: beasts, magnolia, sycamore
screaming in the feral night. Her girls laugh
on the other side of glass,
long hair wind-whipped
over silent mouths.

Out the window, white mud layers
in chains of dry hills
seal in 65 million years.

Pit Stop: Kipling

The morning after
her wedding she locked
herself in the bathroom.

Meadowlark invisible,
spilling its riddled trills
on cow shit.

Visiting Grandmother

Eighty-five, she pours tea,
serves chokecherry sauce
squeezed years ago from fruit
down the lane. Sits and rocks,
watches her granddaughters leap
through the sprinkler, watches

her daughter who just left
husband, farm, brick house built to last
by his ancestors, watches
this woman not touching her cake,
keeping herself like silverware
in a glossy, wooden case.

Rose

A round they used to sing
around the campfire:

Rose, Rose, Rose, Rose
Will I ever *see thee wed?*
I will marry at thy will, Sire,
At thy will...

How is a song round?

One part begins again
before the other's done, the vet sighs, it never ends.

Twin calves suckle in a roadside slough.
Rose, Rose, Rose past Lake Manitou.

Two horses

in a field, heads
interlocked. Each one rests
on the other's neck and mane.
They are not lovers. They can hold
this pose for hours.

Thunder in the distance, veins of a storm.

Nut Mountain

In the motel, after breakfast,
she notices her hand lighter,
bare of its wedding ring.

Finds it later, bright between
the sheets of her unmade bed.

Denn alles Fleisch, es ist wie Gras...

the vet sings along,
remembers the famous conductor
now long dead, the calves
in her hands gasping for breath.

Laughter from the back, music,
the scene always changing
as long as she drives.

Poplar's new green, white trunks slim
as teenage girls, rise
and rise to the dirge.

"Denn alles Fleisch, es ist wie *Gras"*: Then all flesh, it is as grass.

Snow Geese

at dawn fly up,
undulate in a silver ring.

This is what she pulled
from her finger, flung
to the sky in her dream.

Climbing

My sister fracturing a slope of snow
with her fall. Minutes ago her bone was whole;
we wanted to summit. X-rays won't show
tips white and distant, afternoon-lit. Her howl.
The helicopter took her. I was left
holding a sleeve. Alone, I folded up
the sky, she descended to stone; lifting
her wrist, impossible at first. Nerve-sleep.
Then speaks in twitches. I can feel the ridge
under skin of metal that will outlive her,
see the summer night she wakes and rides
the tingle of a healing line, the scar
she's climbing with a fingertip to numb
terrain, receding down the slope again.

LIVING ROOM

We view the pure white falls, not what is crushed
in old canoe trip slides. Nistowiak
is pitching from the wall, its torrent caching
all we did beside it decades back:
Mom frying ham, my brother flicking stones
into the foam, christening me with names
I still hiss at the mirror. Where do those stones
exist? One autumn by a broken dam,
I'd pick them up from the debris, ascend
a face of rock once veiled by water. Cheekbones,
cracks from the old pressure. Climbing depends
on loving the rock wholly and letting go.
Next slide: I'm laughing in the Rockies, age three,
a precipice, a glacier crowning me.

Peonies (Paean)

"Great-Grandma in her Garden," c. 1952. Black and white photograph.

She leans a little over the magnificent blooms
so that her hair—white, wavy in a loose bun, illumined
by the sun—blooms above them. Saskatchewan. June's

end, likely, because the lilacs behind her are done,
the soil pebbled and thirsty. She's raised these down
on her knees, seasonally taking a knife to the dense,

encroaching leaves to prevent diseases caused by lack
of air. If a plant touches another, she cuts it back
and after heavy rain she's out, of course, with stakes,

lifting, tying, supporting all that extra weight.
Such a fine exuberance is usually a sign that the roots
were dug in decades ago, possibly when, uprooted

from Germany, my family settled here. She was ten.
And these blossoms will live past the one who bends
as a physician attending her petals of milky skin.

Sea Change

My blanket
I want to touch it
Forever
—SOPHIA

The consonance you summoned at age two,
touching *it* to *blanket,* the t edging
forever and silence in my room as you
napped that winter afternoon. What ages
passed before you woke? Your smile—antique
and wise as if you'd seen me in the mirror
at thirteen, seen inside my eyes a ticking
beast I couldn't name, that disappeared
into your turning on my bed. I turned
into you turning on my bed. For a minute
I was two, carelessly touching a worn
blanket, flowing, seamless, infinite.
Now you're thirteen, thousands of miles away.
I'm older in my room. We're fixed that way.

Mrs. H.

Nonsense, another jam-jam's good for you
and my freezer's loaded for a year or two
with maple fudge, date pinwheels, petits fours.
Just help yourself. The ones next door before
you, now, could eat! I never saw the like—
what those boys devoured! I'd send a cake
wolfed down, I'm telling you. Before my eyes
those kids grew up. Summers, weeding, I'd spy
on water fights and prisoner's base, their cheers
and laughter going on till night. Their tears—
children!—you'll find out soon enough the joys
and torments. Gathering stuff (plus the boy
who always fought), the Mrs. closed the door.
Just me and cabbages. I would see more,
sometimes, through lit-up windows or the chink
my mind would make removing bricks to look
inside: a tucking-in; a dream begun.
You think I'm strange! But look around—just grainy
photographs and furniture; life happened
there. It seemed their easy happiness
was bread and butter, yet... well, you know a house
is seldom what it seems. The main thing is,
they were like family (to a degree;
the benefit—it's like watching TV—
if it doesn't suit, a news broadcast or scary
show, you switch it off and go upstairs

to bed). More tea? So soon? Not feeling well?
I'm not surprised; the date so close, your swell
looks fit to burst. You must take these. I trust
you'll find the door. At dusk, I never trust
those stairs. Forgive. To tell the truth, my sight's
not what it was. Cataracts, I fear. I'll just sit
here, watch you all the way across my lawn
till you've opened up the door and gone in.

Three Scars

Wrist

Green, rippled water
glass a small girl carries,
slips—

falling water,
bloody shards. *Daddy.*
He stitches so the years
leave, above veins,
a white bridge.

Chin

Children skating in a line
"crack the whip" so the end-

one skids in an arc,
lets go; shooting star
thumps on ice.

How slowly blossoms
red to white.

Arm

Humerus in five
pieces; boats with messengers
from the homeland set

loose, pulled downstream to circle
the whirlpool above mad falls—

Athabasca Falls, 8:40 a.m.

We're here,
early for a change. Still, we didn't beat the rush
already spilled
from minivans, buses, and rental cars into
the rainbow mist below. Be careful not to stray past
the railings; some have,
the brochure says, and died.

Behold—
our cameras, efficient and tiny!
We can pose
endlessly, waste not, delete
all closed eyes, goofiness, bird-shat-on clothes,
and view, endlessly, ourselves
viewing the view, with screens
designed to perfectly capture

this morning—
white beast roaring, unseen, away.

UTILITY ROOM

A precipice, a glacier crowning me
then vanishing as Mom folded the hinge
to stow the counter. Poof! Into the laundry
bin on wheels. I rode as Empress, arranging
subject socks; unlatched the sideways door
above the stairs into a drawbridge; drew up
my lands into tight carpet squares, a board
for chess. My family moves within the rooms.
Bishops and Kings, we watch TV, attack-
wrestle *(it's just a game!),* retreat. Years pass.
What have I become? The house would know. It's tracked
 nightmares, footsteps, pressures, prayers, and has
me locked inside a dim place at its core,
the room where I was Queen no longer there.

EMPRESS

The idea of a crown began running in my head then like a tune.

—CATHERINE THE GREAT

Of a Terrible Weight

Eyes brilliant, their look fascinating and glassy,
the expression of a wild beast.
A long and terrifying future is written in them.
When she comes close I recoil, for she frightens me.
—CHEVALIER D'EON

Dogwood, chestnut, lilac, ash, blooming
white all over town. I drive past that lavish
dogwood at dusk and see the Grand Duchess, sixteen,
in her wedding dress of *a silver moire, embroidered*
in silver on all the hems, and of a terrible weight.
Not seen by so many mowing the grass.
Mowing, all over town, droning, they also miss
the girl up the hill in her room lying
on the bed, searching for herself in the glass,
eyes brilliant, their look fascinating and glassy.

Catherine read Tacitus, Montesquieu, Voltaire
for hours, years in her Summer Palace rooms.
They were badly furnished in red damask, she wrote,
I knew I would feel lonely in them. Suicide
attempted, except the knife couldn't penetrate
her corsets. Other confines: the spectacles, feasts,
and toys of her simple husband, the whims and orders
of the Empress, *the weight oj the crown and the jewels...*
a headache, says the girl, *I'm fine.* But in her eyes twists
the *expression of a wild beast.*

Dogwood, chestnut, lilac, ash. Almost May,
nothing is dead. That chestnut is an empire—
two hundred gilded coaches set off across
the snow for the newly acquired Crimea. Inside
the mind of Empress Catherine flourish
dreams of conquest, a blossom a minute.
The girl pulls the blind and eyes the pills.
They're light as blossoms. Pale eyes
promising a journey beyond her body's limits:
a long and terrifying future is written in them.

After survival is the worst, she thinks.
Doctors and parents agog, waft of hospital
everywhere, questions, casseroles, eyes
on her, even at night, as if she's in a book
a woman reads by computer-light, noting
the fireworks staged by King Poniatowski
to celebrate the arrival south of Kiev, or are those
just the lilac next door, my mind swelling
with terrible plans? (Ash, ash is all I see...)
When she comes close I recoil, for she frightens me.

Going to the Sun

Amid hope, amid passion full of feelings,
my fortunate lot has been broken, like the *wind,*
like a dream which one cannot halt:
her love for me has vanished.
—PETER ZAVADOVSKII

Gifts Catherine lavished on her dismissed lovers:
4,000 serfs in Belorussia, a silver dinner service
for sixteen, 50,000 rubles to last till year's end,
a jewelled walking stick not unlike this ditch thick
with Indian paintbrush, butter-and-eggs, pearly
everlasting. Zavadovskii lasted a year. *With extreme feeling*
I accept your affection! she wrote, *I love you like a soul.*
Mist dissolving bit by bit. Summits exposed, and hanging
valleys, ancient, glacially cut above water falling
amid hope, amid passion full of feelings—

last night in perfect silence we made love
in the tiny tent. Afterwards I dreamt I was kissing
a poet in a distant city, an old flame. How potent
the imaginary lover, who insists on ascending
this road called Going-to-the-Sun (behind
you, lost ahead in rainbow and cloud) in my mind,
domain unseen I hope by old stone
walls and weeping walls and towering Dusty Star,
Little Chief. Seen, will I wake someday to find
my fortunate lot has been broken? Like the wind

love flutters Catherine's list of men, whispers
My *Beautiful Golden Pheasant, Vesuvius,*
Saltykov, Ermolov, Zubov... one by one pulls
them into her gilt-edged chamber,
drifts away quiet as it came. Love not
fixed, I envy her this. No guilt—
I'm shovelling snow or on my knees
scrubbing the kitchen floor when I'm
entered and kissed and licked and felt
like a dream which one cannot halt

and somewhere seed is spent—Indian paintbrush,
silky lupine... so lush this might be a dream.
Except for the solidity of road under
me, the difficulty of its construction, 250 tons
of explosives blown in excavation, stonemason falling
400 feet to his death, crews suspended from rope and lashed
by weather, removing snow by hand each spring
so work can begin, you riding the crest
of this, unable, I hope, ever, to say (as you vanish
now over the Continental Divide): *her love for me has vanished.*

Woman on a White Horse

What do you say to a Czarina
mounting horse and marching
at the *head of 14,000 men*
to dethrone her husband?
—HORACE WALPOLE

She came from the blue half-light.
She was snow spun high off a drift
by the wind, woman on a white horse
on my way to school—there!—
see her hair, sabre, a glitter in the air
cast orange by the lights of the arena.
If I'd mounted, then, ridden that current,
snowy empire between my thighs.
I was ten, could only stare at her face—suspended, serene.
What do you say to a Czarina?

She disappeared, of course.
I grew older; her cloak fell,
the park seemed reduced
to a chessboard square. Down
a tiny sidewalk past toy house,
toy garage, toy skidoo, even the church
seemed minuscule. Days at my desk
I dreamed of pushing past
the town's borders, of marching,
mounting horse and marching.

Where did she go? To St. Petersburg
with orders for fleet and troops, to quell
a revolt, strategize, debate with her ministers
on Poland and Turkey, rendezvous
with a lover, all the tasks of an empress!
In our rink, the Carnival Queen, chosen
for beauty, skill, or ability to sell
raffle tickets, skated her round with roses,
crown. I thought she was the one I'd seen
at the *head 0/14,000 men.*

But under one man, our town's
queen cried again and again.
When she found the courage to leave
with her sons, he took them for a weekend
and shot them, one by one.
Woman on a white horse, send
in your troops. Send them one morning
to knock on that door, say the time
has come to reclaim her children and
to dethrone her husband.

Manifesto

We allow and give Leave for all Foreigners to come into Our Empire,
the *vast Lands, unexhaustable Treasures hidden in the Bosom of the Earth-*
to settle in the open Fields, in Colonys or by Places,
to build themselves up Churches with steeples for Bells.
—CATHERINE THE GREAT

You made me when you stepped from the sleigh into the snow.
Moscow unknown to you, fourteen, foreigner about to meet
the Empress. Your mother and you, *six weeks on the way...*
the journey... long, very tiresome, and harrowing. With swollen feet
about to meet a husband who turned gargoyle
and strange. The palaces—prison. Nights, the fire
spat German syllables—*Liebchen,* your father's goodbye
as the coach bumped away. Homeless, you built
houses of words. Empress, you opened this door:
We *allow and give Leave for all Foreigners to come into Our Empire.*

On your steppe my people unloaded doctrines, deacons,
history of persecutions. Industrious. Neat. You prized
them like colonies of pearls. Safe in the orchard, hymn, home,
tight little village turned in on itself,
a man sitting by the fire might hear it rupture—
just wood caving in—but in that, the future: births
and births forward, Aunt Mary's voice on the tape, telling
about the revolution, mid-story, falters. I pressed pause.
She couldn't go on. Her table laid for *faspa* set forth
the vast, lands, inexhaustible treasures hidden in the bosom of the earth
madrigal of aspen and grasses by the river, a whole ravine
in a spoon of Saskatoon jam. Beet pickles, *ikra,* platters
of sausage and ham. What settled among us, then, sifted past
the clatter of dishes and chatter? Dusk, summer,

frog chorus through the open window as we said
grace—she ladled, poured, replenished, her face
suffused with suffering and love. Family around
a table. I wanted more. You made me when you stepped
from the sleigh into the snow, not by letting us
settle in the open fields, in colonies or by places

I've never seen. Wrote Voltaire, *You are... the brightests*
tar... Not fixed for my gazing on your heroic
furthering of my people but a spinning
nebula compressing to ignite motion: a step,
a coup, coronation, a strangling, building, razing,
burning, journeying on, over the Dnieper's rills
to Moscow or by car to Great Deer over the old Borden bridge
(collapsed now) to stand by Aunt Mary's grave.
Even here presses the stellar wind,
building up churches with steeples for bells.

Catherine Reborn

She is a star, and a star she will remain.
She will be neither onion, nor cat, nor golden calf.
She will not be among the gods that are eaten,
she is among those who give food...
—VOLTAIRE

She inherits perfect pitch, the rarest
gift, can pluck B-flat from air, a train's
whistle, the preacher's drone. She's a teen
bored in the service except for notes rising,
falling along the hillocks of a long hymn
in a plain church on the Midwestern plain.
Stubble out the window like a maze
she follows to that speck moving beyond
her gaze, her fingers pressing the pane.
She is a star, and a star she will remain

although her people mistrust girls rising
to the top. Suspect also is her cello—
between her legs an elegant fine wood
she strokes into music too much a spectacle,
like jewellery, too ornate for church. She prays
God will forgive her loving too much the scarf
of sound wrapping her daily, the reins she holds
in certain passages, the notes she rides
galloping, glimpsing other facets, lives.
She will be neither onion, nor cat, nor golden calf

applauded but not worshipped on the stage,
hair knotted under the net prayer covering
her elders insist upon. Yet never caged.
She builds an empire from within, wins
a doctorate against nerves and Beethoven,
her own people. Begins the explorations:
music of Africa, Asia, the histories
of hymns. She crosses bar lines,
spans continents (and won't be forgotten,
she will not be among the gods that are eaten)

thumbing the mbira's keys into its ghostly
music upon which ride her former self
and her ghostly imperial fleet and all
the hunger that domain incurred, all this is fallen
into the Black Sea, swath of dark water
becoming the gap between her teeth, a field
the Africans have called beautiful. See
it as she raises her arms to give the crowd—
thousands—music. They will be filled.
She is among those who give food.

KITCHEN

...the room? Where I was Queen? No longer there,
Mom says of college days. I watch her hands
punch down the risen dough. Shape loaves. Butter
the steaming heel for me. I watch four hands,
the clock's and hers, never resting, changing
pork hock to soup, egg whites to snow, slicing
minutes to seconds, the loaf to a taste so vital
I hate to swallow it. *Sacrifice*
is on my tongue because she rose at six
to knead the bread, she's touched that wooden spoon
so many times she's *in* the spoon, the mixing bowl
slowly cracking. The walls and all this room
will crumble. Warning lapses in the clock—
a stillness in the hands I hate to watch.

Sestina for the Sweater

One sleeve left. The rest has taken sixteen years,
begun in college for the boy who played
the violin. I was so young, just learning to cast
on, cast off, purl two, knit one. I'd lose
stitches, alone in the pew while he filled
the dark church with Sibelius. By 3 a.m., needles

forgotten, wool tangled on the floor, I'd knead
his shoulder for the secret of his gift. In a year
or two, I thought, we'd marry. But I wanted to fill
the sweater with another shape, and played
with his tears in wool, on wood. I chose another I knew I'd lose
even while he held out his hand, sun casting

brilliant shapes down the grave we leaned against. I cast
off guilt and stitches: a new armhole. Needles
of pine, King Lear, warm beer, his loose
way of walking I'd follow in and out of years
and off and on, gaps alone when I'd knit a ply
of my hair into the cuff. When I filled

my bag and left, the last time, grief filled
up my elbows and knees; I broke my wrist. The cast
kept me from knitting and playing
the violin. Too many mistakes. I stuck my needles
in a bag, safety-pinned the sweater from unravelling. That year
I found another I could never lose,

except we kept saying goodbye. But loss
I could count in days, by rows, measuring when next we'd fill
a week or two with love and edgy sports. In the years
to come I'd stitch shoulder to neck, the cast
of our future green with the need
for acreages and children. The sweater matched his eyes. I played

at this, outgrew it. One sleeve left. Sibelius playing
on the radio, I drive through rain, count the lost
strands of their lives, what it would take for my needles
to knit it whole. For whom? (Not my husband, he'll fill
my life. Besides, it wouldn't fit.) But to recast
myself into the sweater done, wool finally touching skin. (Years

later, one tries it on, plays with a cuff, finds my hair, refills
his coffee, feels the loss, casts
me off, casts me on, sound of needles as we face the years—)

He Receives Her Wedding Invitation

She leaned over this handmade paper,
moistened a sponge to draw a line
with water so the weave under
her hands would part. She heard rain's

onslaught at the window and cats
in heat calling from the night's core,
where she was, measuring the mass
of paper into squares. There was no port,

no ocean in it but the colour
under her hands would surge from slits
in the cliffs she'd walk homesick, colour
she kept smoothing taut as sheets,

that stained her fingers. She thought
of me. The blackberry, house of thorn
I offered in the rain, fruit
dangling up in confused dormers

unpicked, our delicate untwining
of brambles yielding no clear aisle.
They left white sickles on her hand.
These like pins of rain as islands

of paper grew, repeated folds
and vows under her breath till dawn.
The final task: she snipped this gold
cord to precise lengths, wrapped one

around the paper fold and knotted
for a bow. Her finger an acrobat
ringed by gold for the second knot.
A quick withdrawal. She pulled it tight.

The Violist Crafts a Pair of Wedding Rings

The molten gold 1 stir recalls
adagio, the sound uncoiling
from my strings in rehearsal

to thicken in the crucible
our ears made. I pour a pool
of this into a mould; audible

gold it isn't, yet could these hands
that have loosed flocks of Haydn's
notes into a hall, imbue a band

of metal with tone? It's red hot,
the hot centre of that concert
my fingers shaped towards the beat

of gulls I sensed above the glass
ceiling that sealed our music. What cries
outside our neat phrases? What chaos

if the cello's heat could've split
that glass, music leaking into flight?
We played a quartet. No gulls in it.

Now I calculate what length of gold
to cut. The ends I take and solder
into a ring I swear will not hold

a finger prisoner. See it dive
under the baby he delivers
blue and will revive.

Hear a sparrow's voice rise
with the glinting hand that lifts and ties
her garden's fallen irises.

Daily

The fork, leaving
my mouth, travels to plate, then sink,
dishwasher, drawer, in your hand
beats eggs in Grandma's bowl.

You cook as though you're still pipetting
DNA. You're always measuring.
As strings sailed us down the aisle,
you checked your watch. Reaching

to set the timer, you make
an egg yolk cataract. There is
the broken bowl, my grief,
you don't know how much,

how many spoons of blood leak
from me each month, amount
of anxiety held while scrubbing egg
from tines. So little time; my fingers

would rather be quiet on the porch
of your eyelashes. That time, obsessed
with BOOP (Bronchiolitis Obliterans
with Organizing Pneumonia), you didn't

see me for days, although we rose,
ate breakfast, faced the sun, felt
the same counter, toothpaste tube—
parallel circuits; calculate

the distance between. The fork is clean.
I'd love to take in
the lovely souffle, but you—
you are the sun

with headlamp in the next room,
holding out a soccer ball, spun
(its axis is your thumb) for our son
into its countless days.

Eclogue at Cobweb Circus

O transient city, shot with sun!

Hanging streets, strung-up facades,
dangling alleys and doors that dim
when the light leaves.
            Then a thousand pillars
appear as air, even to alert travellers
strolling by, as invisible residents
perform the impossible—
            pirouette in a silken hoop,
the high wire,
            hurling down
on the triple trapeze,
            and the tedious feat,
the quiet quotidian: constructing a web.

Returning home, I stop
on the threshold—
            thrumming without sound,
a spider spins at the centre of her act,
vortex like a veil. Uninvited, I stay,
watch the weaving of a web.

First thread a bridge she balances
on, then the laying
            of a loose line,
attaching another, around which Y
she circles, setting out
            spokes to the sun,
streets to a junction, radius rails
to the hub. *Hello,* I try, ignored—

she's embarked on an epic crossing,
slow spiral over the fences and bridges
of her country, circling out to the edge,
sticking her silk, stronger than steel.

A little light left.

Motif of the cupolas, arches ascending.

Theatre throbbing with architecture—
frozen music, from the body emerging
a liquid silk that
            solidifying, limns
the attention, even after sound.

September was grass
silvered with discs. Close-up,
an orb web
          orbited me back
to a city by the sea, Circular Road
where I'd wandered, wishing I lived
in those majestic mansions. *My mind*
carried the exquisitely crafted doors,
panels of prismatic, bevelled glass,
so from the grass, gently,
          I lifted the piece, replaced a pane;
a perfect fit.

An office overlooking a garden.
I was writing away my *lemures*—
family phantoms for the most part—
when glancing out, glimpsed larvae
riding along lines of silk;
rising,
          sinking, as if using circus wire
or cables to climb
          and plummet.

Diamondback moths, larval,
feeding frenzied underneath
leaves, let out lifelines if disturbed;
retreat, renew; then return to the feast.

Back to my battle, breaking to watch,
apparitions all afternoon.

Moments remain. Move forward:
tomorrow, same time and location.
Cathedrals for breakfast,
            rose windows
from a thread. If the wind tonight
blows the centre apart
            (Dresden, New York,
torn shadows)—
            spiderlings will balloon to the edges
of intricate forests; caravans, troupes
raise up the big top in another vacant lot.

BOYS ROOM

(Mrs. *H.)*

A stillness in the hands I hate to watch—
the neighbour kids on Halloween playing
dead. I gaze up anyway as the witch
in the window rises, kisses the little queen
to life. Swords, pirates, pillows, Dracula
storm back, battle behind the glass in silence;
where is she, her crown... ? Behind my callas,
among toy cups and dill, I found her once
carving rooms in the dirt with a stone. I turned
cold, watching, and thought: *Her house*
will never keep the chill away. I turned
away, I can't explain. Now Dracula's pushing
her again. Lights out. A new game: Murder
in the Dark? I'm all alone and safe down here.

THREE BROTHERS

Nemeiben Lake

i.

We are all night
on the rock, not cold,
talking. The birch, stripped
to a white heart, releases

a skeletal leaf.
How you couldn't breathe
in the log cabin behind us,
wheezed as Dad grasped

for the syringe. You'd laughed
too hard. Listen: the loons
set off chains of laughter,
the moon is choked with ash,

your dreams said unlatch
the iron door in our basement
brick wall and enter, enter
the ash chamber, remains

of all our family fires,
birch burning, Sunday noons
the blue lung flames collapsed.

ii.

Ancient tunnels
in Cairo, dust
muting footfalls,
City of the Dead:

sarcophagi, stone
so hot to touch
your fingers, torches,
lit peepholes to rooms

where a boy, trapped
in our basement, building
a Lego tower, might shed
the air, march upstairs

for milk. That boy,
tickled, pinned
beneath another,
older, on the landing,

(rug worms imprinting
his cheek) loses himself
in laughter, says *I am*
this vessel stuffed

with laughter, suffering
for breath, and breathes,
leaves the tunnel by
a fissure in cement

to his father's workshop.
Plays there in cedar
and cherry dust as the band saw
casts a watchful eye.

iii.

Grey dawn, grey
lake, grey rock.
The moon, not cleaving
to the night or cleaving

night from day, rolls
up our sleeping bags
along that sleeve
of black spruce. On this rock

you'll give your heart
to another in the heart
of winter's breath and
birch and moss and skin.

Flight

Embers smoulder under sand,
coals criss-crossed with lights I send
up with a stick. I watch a city
below extinguished with each hit.

Over Montreal, my brother
prepares to land. He will ensure
a perfect descent. Hazy fire,
late sun on the St. Lawrence far

as the yard from his childhood room:
garbage burning, August, his dream
to find an opening and run
touchdowns, touchdowns past the arena,

cement yard, graveyard, town limits,
into the sky where he'd meet
an older self descending. At thirteen
he saw himself: checking routine

lists, *flap selected, one hundred above,*
the runway lines brief
as clover under his feet. *Sixty knots.*
Control locks. Down.

My stomach knotted
on the six-block plod to school: steeple,
roofs, bricks, hedges, crabapple
bashed on the sidewalk. I tightroped
the cracks and a leaf became a ripped

sleeve fluttering in the ditch outside town
where the girl's body was thrown, a stained
scrap the police missed. I dared
another glance down, saw the murdered

girl's grave dug by ants; she was picked up
in all the sidewalk's pocked
corners. My walk took years. I teetered
along that high-wire way in terror

of passing trucks, of one step
off the line. Was he intercepting
footballs? Over the line at twilight
was my brother falling like the lit

tips of waves that mesmerize
years later, waves that might erase,
as they run toward me on the shore,
this city of embers? Perhaps his hair

carried fire at dusk across a field,
the screen door slammed, the bathtub filled-
I can't remember him. That summer
he must have slid his hand down the same

banister I did, heard that squeak
of wood under moist palms, the clock's
faint heart. He brushed the hallway wall
as we had our mother's womb.

Wail
of a night train—the murdered girl
was in his class. He heard a gale
stirring acres above us as I
heard her. On the spring day

he climbs out of St. John's and reaches
cruising speed, I approach
a footpath in that city. He flies
to Gander and returns: one flash

for all of my steps by the river,
weight of bags, dog shit jumped over,
stone by stone the high tower revealed
at the rate of my slog up the hill.

Waves toss up their burning wings,
feathers, even harp strings to the waning
sun that seems closer than the plane
above, drone familiar as wind. I lean

back, listen to it cross the Gulf.
It drags an unsayable grief:
If he should, if he—
                                                                      He lifts
his two-year-old son, who laughs

to be tilted so high above the rug
and his father's chin, who trusts the rigging
of his father's arms and sees no map
below, only the chest he topples

in giggles against, and begs for more.
Supper. Uniform in the mirror
checked. Schedule: Halifax to Boston,
back by midnight. His son

falls asleep, his wife is rocking
in her chair, timing each creak
to the little breath, little rise and fall.
I skip a stone and watch it fall.

Passages

My tears have been my meat.
—PSALM 42

i. Running

Lightning, bone shatters.
In the ditch flash
thistle, brown-eyed Susan,
a closed rose. Dog's growl
of thunder. Bone shatters,
sky opens. Spotlights
the gravel road and something
else, a scene I'd rather not—

You came to us when I was two.
Your mother drank. Your father played hockey,
was famous, maybe, you'd never

seen him. In the dark cabin at Waskesiu
when you were five and we were new
I was hungry, cried. Mom came to me.

You couldn't sleep, tiptoed to the room,
stood in the hall, watched her feed me.
There was a moon. It made a line

across the sill you didn't cross.
How long did you stand
hidden, cold, hating?

Devil on my back, downpour:
no breath, no light, no white
farmhouse ahead. Torrent
of grief and wet.

ii. House

Here we were contained.
Not in the yard—caragana's
scratch and bloom framing

our games of kick-the-can,
when you ran up and booted
that thing harder than anyone,

freeing us from prison, hooting,
pushing me in victory.
Not in the rink—the shots

against you in goal, glory
of a save or the puck slipping
past you, my prayer, the roar.

Not in the town's net ripped
in two—Indian, White,
you caught between—or in the lap
of Dad, the weight
of spankings and his rule.
But in a room not light

where fear was born. Through
the walls came the faint scratch
of bats and my breath flew

away leaving a mass
on me I couldn't heave,
the house wouldn't take back.

iii. Christening

Our parents sold the house.

We drive north
to the Muskoday Reserve
Anglican Church to see
your three daughters baptized.

In the graveyard, plastic and real
violets, everywhere wild strawberry,
small, unripe.

The moon by the altar
has been rendered in oils
full and clear above
Christ and the children.

I love this girl,
your daughter.

It is meet and right so to do.

She lifts her face to meet
the water, smiles
as it falls down her cheek.

STORAGE ROOM

In the dark I'm all alone and safe, down here
in cedar closet smell and furnace purr,
with boxes of stuff and dust. A cracked mirror
lines my face so an old woman peers
into the room. Reads foolscap sheets crowded
with crooked q's and e's, then words, stories
and poems I wrote. Fur hats, a wedding gown,
journals *(why does he hate me?),* feelings stored
like plums in jars. My family laughing, dancing
in a circle. My cousin's ashes, the blue spruce
crushing my uncle. Another death; I bring
the body here, wait years. How this space
opens to stars and beating heart, selves
the mirror's cracking silver saves and saves.

House (Reprise)

i. Christmas Eve

No one, it seems, is home, except
a dog barking in the garage,

the only sound at driveway's end
where galaxies, hoarfrost flaking

off branches, icicles, a million
silent things keep watch. Hidden

from view, under snow, around
the back, our initials wait for spring

when someone coming down the steps
might puzzle over a muddy

sidewalk palimpsest and never
know the summer afternoon

we scratched them in; wet concrete's
delights; I was too young to see

that it would set. They've removed
the vines. The dog's upset. Street light

is writing on a fingerlet
of ice the names of everything

I can snap off and turn away
holding walking as it melts

ii. Inside

Whose house is this I thought I knew?
Who shrunk it? How came bric-a-brac?
What cruel joke turned once palatial
rooms into a pawnshop-funhouse-
florist's three-in-one? I've walked
through mazes, find no wizard but
a clown. My room's a boy's. He keeps
hamsters and stripes. Gone are the islands
of my rug; gone too, the goddess
printed on my sister's sheet,
whose face—it was just flowers, I think—
haunted the hours I lay in bed.
She wore a wreath, was watching me
and not. Years back, I saw her in
the moon at Trinity; same eyes,
slanting and sad, running mascara,
same lips parted to smile or snarl
depending on the way I stood
in fog. Steam from someone's shower,
appointments. Grandma thinks it's time
for me to go. Goodbye. Thank you.
You've done wonders. What? The doorbell's
still the same? You'll let me try.

Yes, still—the eerie chime. Slides past
the door to me alone, outside.

iii. Brickyard Ruins

This field, the expert said.

In thistle gargantuan, much larger
than me, I'm unarmed
(bare skin, not even repellent
to fight the swarms),
look for shards,
an outline, trace.

Advance prairie storm.

No time; a baby wails,
I've come too far. In the hammering
rain, my old doctor offers
unshelled fresh peas I clutch
as lightning roots
the field in reverse.

My small town's kiln wasn't
after all the elegant dome with light
pouring through the door.

Scove kiln:
just a pile of unfired brick
not unlike
the one my son works
in the backyard, tongue to lip,
utterly absorbed

in pulling wagonloads,
mixing dirt and water. All
afternoon, all summer he's everywhere
and here, stuffs in dried poppy stalks
(seed pods rattling), breathes
on these for fire.

Annular

The wedding ring is lost in the *grand piano*

gold in the lonely
notes of Satie's
last compositions—

(scores found
after his death
in pockets of suits,
umbrellas, webs).

Technician's report:
No buzzes, clicks—
mysteriously inaudible.

lost 198,000 miles from earth

escapes out
the hatch, slips
one astronaut's
grasp, flipping
into the silence
(alone weightlessly
tasting the stars)
tumbling, hits
another's helmet

ricochets per-
fectly back
down its path
into the craft
onto the hand
down to earth
captured in the atmosphere
back to Houston,
back to the suburb,
the ring stares
at that orb
betrayed, cursing
the moon is no door.

of her annulled marriage, lost

perhaps in
the Florida house,
ring non-existent
except when she's
at the hairdresser's
watering the plants
playing canasta
vacuuming the stairs
making a casserole
or love, beautifully,
a penny for your thoughts,
he asks. *Nothing,*
she laughs, *nothing.*
lost *at* the bottom *of a pond near Millersburg, Ohio*

was not blessed
by elders convinced
an earthly treasure

could distract
the congregation from
heavenly pursuits.

This tripled its worth
to the one diving
into the impossible
murk again,
desperate for the world
in so much ooze.

Sifting through bags of leaves for the lost ring, the couple converses:

—after your illness—
—raking, shovelling—
—in the *hydrangeas?*
—compost? cosmos?

—in thirty years
someone digging
our garden in April—

Dusk, hands
too cold
to look further.

The wedding ring, removed before surgery,

is pocketed by
her husband who
leaves to sing.

He'll recall
rushing, changing
into his tux, smoothing

trousers, thinking
about cancer,
failing to hear

the falling ring.
Falling where?
The hole, darkened

hall that took
his voice that night,
motet by Bach—

Unser Leben
ist ein Schatten
(Our life
is a shadow).

four times lost on a farm near Carmel, Saskatchewan

cleaning grease
from his hands
at the straw pile

(she searches for days,
meticulously, finds it)

feeding chickens

(at a gopher's hole
the following spring
she picks it up)

plastering the smokehouse

(after a year
tethered to the
weathered wall)

dying (too loose
he puts it away;
after the funeral
she combs the house
for years, lights
on a box, opens
to gold in a bit
of afternoon sun,
the old music—

Graveyards

To My Cousin

Phone call. You'd died. I didn't cry. Attended
Mozart's *Requiem* instead, heard
cellos in fog, footfalls of the dead. My head

was full of jealousy—raining, a curse—
of a friend who, minutes from your corpse,
was receiving coveted honours; her four-course

dinner and your husk lay side by side,
a gulf away from me and close. Inside
the basilica, the voices swelled inside

my mind; thoughts of Mozart, how he'd left,
at 35, this music incomplete.
They threw his body, bagged, into a pit.

Requiem left in fragments—phrases
filled in by someone else. I thought, what price,
desire. It was consuming me, and the precious

years slowly wasting your body. Tears
came in the *Lacrimosa... tearful that day...*
where Mozart stopped. I was remembering

how months before, at my wedding, you came
over, stooped (I was honoured you'd come
at all), whispered that I was fucking beautiful.

Twillingate Stone

I wish I could marry this son who died
at twenty-one, and his view of icebergs,
whales, fishing vessels, gulls, distant
islands, sunsets, planets, the moon.
Capering waves, wind, our realm
in storm turning to foam and frenzy,
then down the twilit green, these stones-
our children running to the sea.

To my uncle

who loved the tree and knew its name that fell
on him, who loved the leaves falling that fall
he died, and his son who, unknowing, felled

that tree in the blinding, late afternoon sun;
uncle who didn't leave after he'd gone
but lingered on, his gentle presence in

the air, among us walking through leaves
to his grave, hovering as if such love
could never leave, leaves falling as we left.

Violet *Cemetery*

come as we go far away
from the noise of the street...

Lyrics he gives to her
in May when love is born
against graves by the river,
old trees, cold pizza, Chaucer-
companions perfect
to the romance she preserves
like a golden pear
even as she marries
another, over the years
still reads his letters,
meets him imaginarily
until one May she returns
to Violet Cemetery;
instead of an orchard
of pear trees, the affair
revealed to her tortured
husband (reading the paper
in the car), she finds a yard
cold as a face at an airport
bar some rainy January.

Old Protestant Burying Grounds

i.

My, how they've let it go!
Stones flat on their backs
as if the last workout were
too much. Look at the cracked
sarcophagi—founders,
mind you, backbones
of the province resting in such
derelict homes. Check
out the names—where names
exist, apparently the record
of burials is incomplete,
the period vague and lacking
accuracy—Penelope
and her sister, of course, racked
by who knows what. Homeless
hide their sleeping bags, broken
carts and bottles, whatnot.
And see that grave knocking
its way, by fallen angles
and angels, into a backyard—
an epitaph, toys, barbeque,
garden blooming from a corpse!

ii.

To find the graveyard
photos, pry the lid off
that Rubbermaid. A mess,
I know. Myself, my house,
and family in our prime.
So tired; you look and I'll
lie down, try to remember.

Churchyard: Tiefengrund

Snow cancels the highway; fields are all.

A few months ago, you
who'd nursed my mother,
watched me nurse.
He's thirsty now,
crying in the back seat.

We who follow the hearse
came from you, who knew
almost a century.

Here is the church.

You who knew this ground
in baby shoes, wedding shoes and all
weather are lowered in
so deep
I can hardly recall my birthday, summer solstice,
when you sat on the beach
watching us release into the water
wreaths of fire.

Now my baby, too cold at your grave,
sleeps, his breathing almost fierce
as we pull away.

Change Islands

So named because I've heard
people here changed
islands by season, wintered

on the South and on the hinge
of spring swung to this North
Island, exposed to the slap

of the sea, then back. No one on the path.
Past small graveyards I sleep
by sea urchin skeletons, give

no thought to the phalanx
of cloud coming on. No grief,
except my pail lacks

the partridgeberries I seek.
In Chaffey's Cove, lobster traps
of broken slats and twine slack

with age, perhaps ripped
by tide, invite my hand inside:
bedroom, kitchen, parlour

where they took bait, and died.
Except the small one who, lured
by herring, tangled in the rooms,

jerked toward a slitted heaven
and found a hatch, a moon
to slip through into a haven

of sea, flux in the gulch, in
and out, applause of water
over stones and surge, again,

again, no house, no mortar,
feast of red-berries, heave
of tide, I believe in heaven, here.

Moving

Constant is the graveyard slanting up behind
the house in a wash of sunlight or in winds
that lash this coast where spruce bend,
lose branches, remain. Father had no words
at the airport but when we moved to the brim
of this country I saw his tears in the stars
splaying down the crevices of cliffs. From
Greenland icebergs travel to dissolve here;
centuries' wisdom is salt I lick from my lip
in a fog. Constant is the moon's yellow eye
on water rushing from a campground pump
into a small, steel bowl I carry to our site.
With each step water sloshes out of bounds,
takes moonlight with it, finds strange ground.

NOTES

The epigraph by Eliot is from "East Coker" in *Four Quartets.* The epigraph by Rilke is from "Dich wundert nicht des Sturmes Wucht—/ You are not surprised at the force of the storm—" in *Rilke's Book of Hours: Love Poems to God,* translated by Anita Barrows and Joanna Macy (New York: Riverhead Books, 1996).

Information on brickmaking in "House" was drawn from the Claybank Brick Plant National Historic Site and Virtual Museum. Frank Korvemaker and his article "History Built Brick by Brick" (North *American Brick),* Larry Buhr and his M.A. thesis, "An Archaeological Survey of Bricks Manufactured in Saskatchewan," and Hilda Maier also provided valuable information.

Richard Thiessen provided information for "My brother's wedding ring," as did historical family books by Katie Nickel Dueck and Woldemar Nickel. Don Coles inspired the form.

Francisca (15) and Angelina (17) Wartenberg, the subjects of Renoir's *Acrobats at the Circus Fernando,* were from an itinerant family of German acrobats and contortionists.

The phrase *"Derm alles Fleisch, es ist me Gras"* from "Road Trip" is from Johannes Brahms' *German Requiem.*

The title words in "Peonies (Paean)" are derived from Paian, a figure in Greek mythology, student under Asclepius, god of medicine. In one version of the story, Paian used the peony to heal a wound suffered by the god Pluto. Asclepius, upstaged, threatened to kill his pupil. Pluto saved his life by turning him into a peony.

The borrowed quatrains for the glosas in "Empress" are adapted from prose material about Catherine found in Miriam Kochan's *Catherine the Great,* John T. Alexander's *Catherine the Great: Life and Legend,* Voltaire's letters, and Catherine's Manifesto of 1763, found in Roger Bartlett's *Human Capital: The Settlement of Foreigners in Russia 1762-1804.* Information was drawn from these sources, as well as from Catherine's memoirs. The opening epigraph and italicized phrases in other than the tenth line of each stanza are Catherine's, from her memoirs.

Empress Catherine II, known as Catherine the Great, ruled from 1762 to 1796, one of the longest reigns in Russian history. With no legal claim to the Russian crown, she overthrew her husband in a coup six months after he became czar. Her guards murdered him a week later.

Frozen music in "Eclogue at Cobweb Circus" is by Goethe: "I call architecture frozen music." *Lemures,* also called *larvae,* were in ancien Rome the ghosts of the dead of a family, considered as troublesome unless exorcised from the household.

Information for "Annular" was drawn from Charlie and Dotty Duke's *Moonwalker* and Michael J. Hepp's *The Legacy of St. Peter's Colony.*

In “To My Cousin,” the first line of the “Lacrimosa” from W. A. Mozart’s *Requiem* is *“Lacrimosa dies ilia”*: Oh how tearful that day..

The opening song lyrics in “Violet Cemetery” are by Natalie Merchant from “Lily Dale.”

In “Churchyard: Tiefengrund,” *Tiefengrund* translates from German as “deep ground.”

“Salmon Cove Point” is for Mary Dalton.

“Sea Change” is for Sophia Nickel.

“Woman on a White Horse” is for Blanche Nickel.

“Catherine Reborn” is for Mary Oyer.

ACKNOWLEDGEMENTS

Poems in this book appeared, often in different versions, in the following periodicals:

Books in Canada: "Moving"; *Canadian Notes and Queries:* "Athabasc Falls, 8:40 a.m.," "Living Room," "Mrs. H.," "Three Scars"; *The Fiddlehead:* "Acrobats at the Circus Fernando," "The Violist Crafts a Pair of Wedding Rings" (originally titled "The String Quartet's Violist Crafts a Pair of Wedding Rings"); *Maisonneuve:* "Change Islands"; *The Malahat Review:* "Flight," "Sestina for the Sweater"; Notre *Dame Review:* "Salmon Cove Point"; *Prairie Schooner:* "Road Trip (originally titled "Ring"); *Rhubarb:* "Manifesto," "Moving."

"Manifesto," "My brother's wedding ring," "Moving," and "Sestina for the Sweater" were published in *Half in the Sun: Anthology of Mennonite Writing,* ed. Elsie K. Neufeld (Vancouver, B.C.: Ronsdale Press, 2006). "Change Islands" and "Flight" were published in *The New Canon: An Anthology of Canadian Poetry* (Montreal, Quebec: Vehicule Press, 2005).

Thanks to the Canada Council for the Arts for a grant that assisted in the completion of this manuscript. Thanks also to the Saskatchewan Writers Guild (St. Peter's), Daphne Robinson, and Sylvie Ingram and Hugh Longhurst for writing space. Heinz and Lois Klassen deserve special thanks for generously providing an invaluable space at a crucial time.

For a decade of commitment to these poems, deepest thanks to Stephanie Bolster and Christopher Patton, without whom this book would not exist in its present form. For insightful critiques, I'm also grateful to my editor, Ken Babstock, and to Elise and Steve Partridge, Mary Dalton, Sue Wheeler, Sue Ann Alderson, Shannon Stewart, and Leonard Neufeldt. Thanks to the Vancouver Poetry Dogs for inspired readings. Thanks to Doris White, Margaret and Tom Bolster, Evan and Janice Kreider, and the late Pauline Giesbrecht for sharing their stories. For informational assistance, thanks to Richard Thiessen, Chris Kent, Frank Korvemaker, Larry Buhr, and Hilda Maier. Thanks to Bevan Voth for patience and support.

Thanks to all my family—immediate and extended—for love and inspiration.

ABOUT THE AUTHOR

Barbara Nickel's previous collection of poetry, *The Gladys Elegies,* wo the Pat Lowther Memorial Award. Her work has appeared in numerous literary magazines and anthologies, including *Notre Dame Review, Prairie Schooner,* and *The Malahat Review. A* previous winner of *Malahat Review's* Long Poem Prize, she was also a CBC Literary Awar finalist in 2004. Also an award-winning author of books for children, she lives in Yarrow, B.C., with her husband and two children.

www.ingramcontent.com/pod-product-compliance
Lightning Source LLC
Jackson TN
JSHW081409170426
101040JS00015B/334

* 9 7 8 1 4 8 7 0 0 0 0 9 7 *